# RISE

"Focus on you, put yourself first and allow the world to wrap itself around the healthiest, happiest version of yourself"

– Michael J. Brue, SR.

# RISE

Discover The Step-by-Step Formula For Success In Real Estate

Without Any Experience

## Michael Brue

Florida

RISE

Tiger Storm Press
1391 NW St Lucie West Blvd, Suite 247
Port St Lucie, FL  34986
TigerStormPress.com

This publication is designed to provide accurate and authoritative information regarding the subject matter covered. It is sold with the understanding that the publisher is not engaged in rendering legal, accounting, medical or other professional services.

The information and opinions presented in this book are intended for educational purposes only.  Any income claims or results discussed in this book are not typical, and they are for example only.

ISBN: 0578541793
ISBN-13: 978-0578541792

Published in the United States of America

# Dedication

I would like to dedicate this book to my late niece, Summer Alexandria Rioux. She passed on just before her 4th birthday in 2000. I know she was little and we did not get much time together but, for all that knew us both knew we had a special bond. She had this amazing energy about her that could give even uneasy adults a calming peace. She used to see the "Rock" Dwayne Johnson on TV and say to her mom, my sister Michele, "that's Uncle Mike", obviously she saw me from a different viewpoint. I know that no one can miss her more than her loving parents but man this little angel now in heaven sure did change all of our lives. Love you Summer Alexandria, you sure did touch and change each of our lives.

"The price of success is hard work, dedication to the job at hand, and the determination that whether we win or lose, we have applied the best of ourselves to the task at hand."

–Vince Lombardi

# What Others Say About Working With Michael

"'The General' AKA Michael Brue! Truly the most influential person I have ever met! I met him at a very low part of my life. He quickly became my friend and mentor. He believed in me, encouraged me, motivated me, when I didn't have the strength or energy to drive forward. One of my favorite quotes from him, "Give me the 30 second version". He is full of Passion, Drive, and most important Integrity. I am forever grateful to have this extraordinary man in my life!

Thank you for continuing to guide me to Break thru the next level. "

Kellie Linder

"Joining Keller Williams in 2015 was a decision that truly changed my life for the better. Thinking that all real estate companies were the same I was, and continue to be, pleasantly surprised because of the difference with KW.

Michael Brue is one of those surprises. Michael is the consummate professional only better.  His all-business exterior is further enhanced with a huge heart that sincerely desires the best. The best that his company can offer, the best tools for the agents to excel, the best service for buyers and sellers and actually, he desires to be the best he can be for his family and beyond. I'm blessed to know him and be part of his team. The total win-win!"

Lynda St Julien

"I have had the distinct pleasure of working with Michael Brue for several years now. Michael has proven to have laser focused ability to set goals and achieve them. One of those years we worked side-by-side as a team on our one thing and completely dominated our goals. He is a fearless leader he cares deeply for his family and his people and like the dogs he loves so much he is fiercely loyal. I will choose him on my team any day. I have said it many times to many people he is the best boss I've ever had. He is also a very dear friend. All the best Michael!"

Julie Phillips

"There's no doubt that you've had the most positive impact on my life. When I walked into your office over five years ago, I was filled with fear that I would not be able to start a new career in my 40s. I shared with you a little bit about my past accomplishments and my tenacity to succeed and it instantly struck a chord with you. You spent the next 30 minutes getting to know me and seeing my unlimited potential.

You didn't just fill my head with clichés about success. You personalized a plan encouraged me to follow the steps to attain my goals. Within a short time, I closed my first few deals and began teaching classes at Keller Williams. You made me feel part of the family at a time of transition where I could've felt lost.

Over the years, you've encouraged me through the crisis, motivated me to persevere and now I'm happy to say that I am thriving in a career that I've grown to love. I never imagined that in my late 40s I would've found my true career path and a dear friend who shares many of the same philosophies and passion for life. I will forever be grateful for

Your ability to always see the best in me and quite actually, the best in everyone. I truly consider you a blessing in my life. You are one of a kind, Michael!"

Michelle Burke

"My personal experience with Michael Brue has been one of a kind and generous person focused on promoting the success and well-being of all. An incredibly energetic professional always thinking outside the box to provide his agents great ideas. Most of all, I think he may be the most loving, sensitive father I have ever known. Grateful to be a dad and proud so show it."

Marguerite B. Krute

"Great men and women inspire those around them to live out their greatness. Michael Brue has a power that few possess, an inner confidence that is intentionally focused on seeing others succeed. Michael is never too busy for a call or text and provides value wherever he goes. Always looking for the Win/Win solution, he has guided me through some challenging situations. He balances family life and work life tremendously. His walk matches his talk, with a high value on Integrity. Thank you for inspiring me!"

Tammy Werthem

"My first meeting with Michael Brue...

It was the summer of 2004 and I remember it like it was yesterday. My mother and I were a very successful team at Coldwell Banker and we were content. It was my mother's 32nd year as a Realtor© and it was my 16th year. My dad had recently retired, and my mom was close to retiring too. We were referred the best-selling author, pastor and motivational speaker, Dr. John Maxwell as a buyer. We were both very excited to meet him and help him with the perfect home in the Palm Beaches. At the same time, several agents in our office switched to the new broker in town, Keller Williams. I didn't know much about them, but I was convinced to meet with Mike the team leader. I was led to Mike's office with expectations of just another broker that wanted more agents. I quickly realized that Mike is like no one else I've ever met. He was surprisingly passionate about life and Keller Williams.  The more he told me, the more skeptical I became. I didn't see how any company could fulfill such promises and expectations.  I remember thinking that if just one of Mike's many claims were true, I would have to join KW. I joined and then broke the news to my mother/business partner. She was devastated and didn't know how I could do this to her. Later that day she was showing the property to Dr. Maxwell and she told him what happened. He asked what company I went to.  When she said Keller Williams, he very enthusiastically replied "touchdown" with raised arms in the shape of goal posts.  He said he knew Gary Keller personally and was the keynote speaker at one of the family reunions. He confidently told my mother to join me at KW right away. Fourteen years later, I realize that every claim Mike made at the first meeting was absolutely accurate and some were understated, and my mother is still working with me! Thank you, Mike, for meeting me and improving my life and career!"

Scott D. Smith, PA


"Michael, the true you is not the hard exterior you choose for the world to see.  It is not truly the pit bull bully dog.  The true you is a passionate caring individual whose passion is sometimes mistaken for arrogance because those people don't possess that type of inner fire cannot see past their own jealousies. The true you has very few in your inner circle and some that believe they are however there are only there for a special purpose or short period of time. The true you loves deeply your family and your faith. The true you doesn't show fear because you analyze it and then conquer it. "

I appreciate the true you because strong people are people to learn from and cherish as a leader."

Cristi Hernandez

"Michael Brue impacted my life before we ever had the chance to speak one on one. I had always considered myself to be a strong leader, but at the time was struggling due to the loss of multiple close family members. Michael came to speak to our office one day and that is when I saw a Leader of Leaders, a man respected and looked up to by everyone in the room. It wasn't what he said that day, but his presence, a motivating and inspirational force that hit me at my core. It was then that I knew, that I did not just want to be an agent, but part of his leadership team, I finally found the Leader, I had been searching for, for years. Since that day Michael has continued to be that Leader and my own leadership abilities have grown exponentially through his guidance. Thank you, Michael."

Steve Banasiak

"Michael, I will be forever grateful for you believing in me! If it were not for you, I would not be where I am in my career in Real Estate today. You take the time to really listen and your advice has always guided me in the right direction. You are not only my Mentor; I consider you to be a valued friend and I am happy to have you in my life! Inspiring and Leading others in a positive direction is a special trait that you have mastered, and I speak for a multitude of people whose lives you have touched. Keep on being you, you are one of a kind!

This was harder than I thought. I kept running on and on this is the version that sums it all up! Thank you for being you!"

Dawn Mansur, PA

"I know Michael Brue as my broker, my mentor, a true involved leader, a coach, a person who inspires everyone he knows, and a person who has my total respect and admiration. I must admit I love Facebook for many reasons, but when I see a post from Michael, I read it. No, not just look at it, but read it and interpret it for my benefit. I know that each and every word is there to encourage and build better, happier, more effective lives. But by far the most important thing I have learned about Michael is he is a real person. A husband, a proud father and a good son and family person. And for me, he is a friend. He tries to help and encourage and his follow through is right on target. He makes everyone feel important. It is with gratitude and appreciation that I take this time to express these thoughts."

Betty Welch

"Michael Brue has taken the concept of time blocking to a whole new level the idea of doing 15 minutes principal is a genius idea any of us can do things in 15 minutes and in real estate once you get the 15 minutes under your belt the next hour is easy and the hour after that it's all about making connections. Michael Brue has come up with an idea to be able to get us motivated add to take ourselves to that next level enjoy reading his book the 15-minute principle and it'll take you to your next level. "

Keith Dean

# Table of Contents

# Introduction

*"If you think you can do a thing or think you can't do a thing, you're right."* – Henry Ford

Welcome to **RISE.**

Inside of this book, I am going to take you on a journey of a brand-new agent that jumped headfirst into this business thinking it would be a walk in the park. I quickly realized that business was not going to be handed to me and I had to find a way to make my own path.

No matter where you are in your real estate career, you can apply the same principles and processes that I have used to build one of the biggest real estate companies in South Florida.

Before we get started, let me ask you this. How many times have you quit in life or maybe in your business? Now before you answer that, I want you to know it is ok. I quit seven times in my first year in the real estate business.

Yes, I said "Seven times I quit". If you've ever thought about quitting because maybe it's not happening fast enough, or you thought about doing something else, it's ok. So did I. I was stubborn, so I hired myself back each time I quit and just kept going again in real estate.

There are usually turning points in your life where you decide on which path you are going to take to move forward. For me, it was back in the year 2000, I was really trying to figure things out and decide what I wanted to do with my life. Then one crazy night I get a phone call from my dad, Michael J. Brue, Sr. Now keep in mind my dad was the toughest man

I knew, so when he called me crying hysterically, I ever knew something major must have happened.

During the first call I could not really understand what he was saying given his condition. But, finally after the second call I got the message, and this quickly became the darkest time in my life. My niece, Summer Rioux, was almost four and she drowned at a lake in upstate New York. I couldn't even believe this was happening at the time. It didn't seem real or even possible to me. How could this happen to Summer.

All I could think was that I needed to get to NY and wrap my arms around my sister and just be there for her. I had a pair of gold boxing gloves on my necklace at that time. I needed to get the necklace to my sister as quickly as possible to let her know to keep fighting. I knew my sister needed support more than anything right then and with that I left * for New York.

With my time away I was able to decide what I wanted to do with my life. Real Estate chose me long before I chose it. It was through this dark season that I got clear at what I wanted most out of this lifetime.

After returning to Florida my dear friend, Gregory Holmes, invited me to an Irish pub. He was instrumental in getting me to make the decision to get into real estate. At that point I quickly signed up for and took the one-week course and passed my 63-hour course test. Then I scheduled my state exam. Bam, just like that, I was licensed in the State of Florida to sell real estate.

Gregory gave me first start in the business on his team at RE/MAX, he later moved his business to Keller Williams. We had an amazing run together in business. The dynamic duo! Brue and Holmes.

Here I am in the first couple months in this business and I am walking around in my office with my name badge on. I think I look pretty good, you know, I was dressed up and I'm walking around and I'm thinking, okay, so where's the business, give me the business. But of course, the business was not just flowing to me. And I couldn't understand why.

Then one day I hear about this seminar with a guy named Rick Ruby. Rick was either a loan officer or a mortgage broker and I think he just spoke so that he could win business for himself. But none the less I decided to attend one of his seminars.

The class starts, and Rick starts talking and of course me being new and thinking I know everything, I start judging him. What does this guy really know that I don't know? But, fortunately for me, I kept my mouth shut and I started to listen to Rick. Then he said something that totally made sense. He said, if you are a real estate agent, why don't you just start talking to people who want to sell their homes.

Then I thought, well, that's brilliant. Why didn't I do that? That was like a revelation that I had all in that moment. Then of course, I thought and asked, well where are these people who want to sell their homes. Of course, he responded, great question Mike, they are for sale by owner people. I thought again, well that's brilliant. So that's what I did. In the rest of this book I am going to show you the process that I used to climb the real estate ladder in the quick manner that I did. I was able to RISE, and you can too!

When I got started in real estate, I didn't have any family in Florida. I didn't have many friends. I didn't have a sphere of influence to speak of. There was nothing that I had to fall back on. There was little to no training on how to get started in real estate. I started my career at RE/MAX, which is a great company, at the time they were the largest real estate company in the universe. So, I thought, well, I should join them, right? Run with the big dogs and everything else we'll figure itself out later. But there was zero training for new agents at that time in the office I joined. If you wanted training, you had to go to outside training events like the "Rick Ruby" type seminars to figure out what it is that you want, need, or must do to become successful selling real estate.

One thing that I quickly discovered was that Rick did not give much direction as to what to say or do with for sale by owner prospects. This is where I had to develop my own system that took me from quitting seven times my first year to quickly becoming one of the top agents in the office for closed units.

There are two sides of a sale that you can be on, the listing side and the buy side. So, buyers are fun, right?

You get to meet new people, put them in your car and show them a bunch of houses. After you get done showing them 15 properties you hope that they like one enough to submit an offer. Then, hopefully the offer gets accepted and the deal goes to close in 30 – 45 days and you get paid.  Not a bad process, but I want to show you the power of working the other side of the street. The listings side of the real estate business.

Listings are somewhat similar, you meet a new seller, view their home, give them a presentation and hopefully list their home for sale. Now the power of the listing is twofold. First, once you add the listing to the MLS (multiple listing service) you have thousands of real estate salespeople essentially working with you to sell that property. You don't have to pay them upfront. In fact, they only get paid if they bring you a buyer and the sale closes.

I want you to see this mindset shift. You can put in the same amount of effort on the front end to acquire a listing as you can to find a buyer a home. The major benefit of the listing is that there is a good chance another agent will bring you a buyer and you still get paid on the listing side. You also may get new buyer leads that are generated from having the listing itself.

Now you might still be saying, Hang on Mike, I love working with buyers and I still want to do that. I say, that is great. As a matter of fact, I'll give you one of the best ways to have an endless supply of all the buyers you want.

Are you ready for the unlimited supply of buyers literally picking up the phone and calling on you? Listings. Yeah, the more listings you have the more buyer phone calls you are going to get.

This is where the idea of teams has become more popular because as a team you can have people that do only listings, while others are just working with buyer clients. It makes sense and the real reason these teams are having so much success is because they are using the law of leverage. They are leveraging their entire business on the right principles. They always start with the listing presentation.

If I have inventory, I can get enough leads, whether they come through the internet or any other source to start now feeding to other agents. By helping buyer's agents, you are creating leverage for your business. You are creating a win because there is a spilt of time and money. As you develop your business more being able to leverage your time by building a team allows you to grow without having to invest more time. Ultimately you want to focus on what you are good at and start building a team around you that will compliment your weaknesses.

The main objective of this opening chapter was to sell you on the mindset and benefit of going after the listing. This will allow you to control your own path in your real estate career. As we move on, I will help you cut through the noise and stay focused on the prize. I have developed a unique system that is the foundation for all the success I have had personally as well as the success in building our real estate offices from nothing to one of the largest in South Florida.

## Setting Up for Success

I can imagine that your time is just as busy as my time. I managed to write one book already and you are reading the second one I wrote now. There are quite a few things going on at any one moment, as I live a pretty full life. Of course, on top of the business I have my kids. Right now, I have one in high school, one pre-teen, and one that just came out of diapers. I am grateful they have a mother who is constantly keeping them up to speed with schoolwork and engaged in sports.

For me to be effective and accomplish everything that I want, I must become skilled at a high level with time management. This is something that I figured out early on.

I'm old school and this was back in 2000. I think it's safe to say I think we were all a little old school at that point. I had an actual calendar that you would open. It had Monday through Friday on it, I would color code my appointments.

## Time Management

The first thing I would do is I would carve in my time management for lead generation and creation time for new business. That was the time where I would block specifically every single day so that I could gain appointments with people. So fast forwarding, today we're talking about listings, which will, by the way, guarantee that you'll be level through any shift, correction or tilt that the real estate market's going to do because those who control the listings and the inventory ultimately control the market in any market. If you control the market with inventory, you can control your time and your money. Who likes these two things? Now given that I know myself, I knew I had to do it first thing. I would schedule time to make the lead generation and creation of leads to be the first thing that I would do in the morning hours of each day.

## The Path to Success

Now I am going to give you my script that I've worked. It's a skit more than a script. I'm going to give it to you. It is what put me on the path for success. In about 24 months I was making close to $200,000 in GCI, selling real estate. I didn't even know how to log into the MLS. I would have to ask somebody in my office to do the computer stuff for me. That's the truth. I knew what I knew and knew what I didn't. Focus on what you know and learn the tech as you go, I did, you can too.

It's one thing to get the psychology of "you need to be on the listing side", but it's another to take the frame of mind to say, "I'm going to actually take the time management skills to carve out that time to do it first, to actually make outbound contact and reach a for sale by owners and listings before they end up with someone else." Now before you think it, because I did at first, let's tackle a common excuse. That is: I'm not sure who I should be calling.

The question then comes up; How do I find these people? Of course, with the evolution of the industry there is more than one way to get a list of people to contact. Firstly, we could use technology and use for sale by owner sites to find potential listings.  There are many sites available with this information, make a list and start calling.

The second way is more old school and the way that I enjoyed the most. We drive neighborhoods and look for the for sale by owner signs and take down their number. You can try to gather as many as you can and then during your time blocked session for calling leads you give them a call.

The goal no matter how you get the list is to have at least 10 people to attempt to contact. That should be your goal for every day of the week. Shoot for at least 10 contacts made during your prospecting time.

By doing this every day you are going to form a habit, and this is one of those habits that you want to have because the success of your business can depend on it.

By making the most of your time, you will eventually start to reap the reward of your labor. The more consistent you are with your time blocking and especially lead generation the more appointments you will get, which of course will lead to more listings. Listings will create ultimate leverage of your time and control of your money.

**Listings = Time & Money**

# Getting the Appointment

I want to give you some scripts for making contact with people. If you get the psychology of this, you've time blocked, you've plugged it in your calendar and now you know who you're going to be calling because you have your lists.

I made most of my money early in the real estate business working for sale by owners. But I do want to give you a little bit of a disclaimer. I believe that this will work as good if not better with expired listings. You just might have to modify the scripts a little bit.

For sale by owners to me are raising their one hand and they're saying, hey, I would like to sell my house. And expired listings are raising that same hand saying, hey, I'd like to sell my house. But they also raised the other hand and are saying, I was listed with a real estate agent, but perhaps we need a different one now because for whatever reason it expired.

I think it's universal and you can use it whenever. When I was contacting for sale by owners, I always have the same script, so I don't have to try to remember these long scripts. I do not have a seven-page written out dialogue for you to remember and master and regurgitate. It's easy and I think if you practice this enough, you'll get it down.

Here is how the conversation would go:

I would call up a for sale by owner:

**Michael:** Hi, this is Michael. I'm with Keller Williams. I was calling to find out if your home is still for sale.

**Seller:** Yes, it is.

**Michael:** Okay, fantastic. I'd love to come and take a look at it. I'm going to be in your area between three and five. When will be a good time for me to come by?

Now before we go onto the next part of the script there's a possibility that they might give us objections right now.

The key to handling any objection is to acknowledge it, absorb it and then keep going.

## Handling Objections

The goal is to acknowledge the objection, absorb it and then move it to the side and just keeping moving towards the goal of getting the appointment. By getting the appointment and viewing the home we now have a chance to build rapport with the seller and potentially get the listing.

I have some real estate agents that make over a million dollars a year selling real estate. Some make $800,000 a year.

Some make $600,000 a year. I have dozens upon dozens that make over $200,000 a year. That's awesome, right? Some are individuals and some of them have teams. Guess what? None of them are so awesome that they can list property over the phone. The first thing that they have to do is they have to get in the door. You have to learn how to go get appointments with people so that you can actually start winning with people. Are you going to do it? Will you make some mistakes? Yes. I'm captain mistake and if you don't think you are going to make mistakes, you will.

It's okay. Go, fail forward. Go make a hundred mistakes. I promise you, inside of 100 mistakes comes about 15 to 20 listings, 15 to 20 listings could give you a small business today.

Are you committed to making contacts with people? Yes? Thank goodness. If you're committed to making appointments with people in contact with people, you're committed to getting those appointments and you say these very easy scripts because you want to come by and take a look.

## Potential Objections

**Do I have to pay a commission?**

Response:
You know what? I'm not sure I'd want to pay a commission either. I just know I'd really love to see your home. I'm going to be in the area today between three and five. What works for you? I want to take a quick 15-minute look at the house. **I have been burned by a real estate professional before.**

Response:
Yep, I could see that you feel you were burned somehow by a real estate agent before, but I know I'd really like to come and look at the house. I'm going to be in the area today between three and five. What works for you? I want to take a quick 15-minute look at the house.

**I am frustrated that five or six agents have already called me.**

Response:
You know what? I can see where you may be frustrated by that. I heard a lot of my colleagues are also calling. I'm part of the inventory team here at Keller Williams, so that would make sense. I'd really love to come and see your house. I'm going to be in the area today between three and five. What works for you? I want to take a quick 15-minute look at the house.

**Do you have a buyer?**

Response:
You know what? I'm glad you brought that up. I work with about 67 families a month at my office through this network / team that we have. And right now, we're out looking at other inventory that's not yet on the open markets, which kind of brings me exactly to this phone call and why I'd like to meet with you. I'm going to be in your area today between

three and five. Do you think that we could possibly set up a 15-minute interview or a run through, so I can look at your house?

**I have friends who are realtors.**

Response:
I totally understand. I have friends who are in real estate too. I'm not sure I'd want to do business with them either, but I know I'd love to come and look at your home. When would be a good time for a 15-minute run through?

Here's the thing, we're doing these objections for you because this is the psychology of it all. They're not all going to give you objections. Maybe you'll get one, possibly even two, but highly unlikely you will get all five objections.

They're simply not that skilled to hit you with all five objections and you're not that skilled to handle all five at once. I want you to think about this for a second. I consider myself skilled, but I do not have the skillset to say no to you like three times in a row. So, don't ask the fourth time because I'm going to naturally cave. I'm powerful at objection number one, two and three.

We are programmed since we were little to say no the first time to almost anything, even stuff that's good for us. It's crazy. But you know what most of you have not been programmed and trained how to say no twice. Very few people are trained to say, no, more than once.

The only objective is to get past the objections and secure an appointment to view the house. Once we are at the house, we can move to the next step of getting the listing.

## Getting the Listing

I want to fast forward you to the actual presentation because I'm assuming that what's going to happen is you're going to get in trouble, and when I say you're going to get in trouble, you're going to get people to say yes to you and then you're going to freak out. You're going to think, oh my gosh, he didn't prepare me for this. They said yes, right? Because you're going to do it a certain number of times and I promise you if you do a certain number of times, you're going to get into a repetitious flow where it's going to make sense. Opportunity will RISE.

Let's move along, right to the point where we get to the home. We get to the home, they've said yes, they've accepted you. Yes, come by and take a 15-minute run through. I think it's important that you remember to bring something to write on, even if you're not old school. Some of you are a real techie, right? You bring your laptops and some of you have your iPads and tablets. Some of you are like tech geniuses but go old school on a listing with a pad of paper and a pen, maybe a clipboard and walk through their home.

I have a little speech when I first come in and I always say:

Hey, you know what? I'm not a listing agent. I'm a little different. I'm a selling agent. I know you probably heard from about six or seven other realtors® who are probably skilled listing agents, but I'm a little different. I'm a selling agent.

You see, I'm networked to the top 20 percent of people who push property in (Your County), and typically we call each other when we're looking for things so that we can find matches quicker. That is why I'm here today, I'm here to look and see if this is something that I can really get sold because I partner with an exclusive few people just like you if we're a match.

So, what I figured we'd do is you would take me on a tour, show me the house just like you would as if I were a buyer. And then after that we can sit down and talk about what it would look like to partner together. Cool.

That's the first close. If they say yes, and they start touring, that's your first close. Now you are kind of in, just don't blow it, right. This is from captain mistake; I have blown more than I've landed.

Now, would you guys do me a favor? Would you tour me through the home as if I were the buyer? Then you can point out all the different things that you've done.  People  love to talk about themselves and they love talking about their home even more.

It will be cool if you have a clipboard and/or a notepad and you're actually taking notes. And by the way, actually take the notes. Don't pretend to take notes.

Take the notes. It's important. You're building rapport with them. You've got them excited. They're touring you to their home. You're taking notes on things that they're saying about the home. I'm just being candid with you. By writing notes you are placing value on what they are saying and starting to build a relationship.

Now we're done with the tour. They want to sell their home. They're excited about it. They're going to be a little passionate about it. They're going to start feeling good because you're there and this is what you do.

Now you need a transition point. You're done. Everybody's feeling good, the vibe is flowing, the mojo's going right. And then we get to that awkward point. We need a transition so that you can comfortably and with confidence say to them:

This is fantastic. This is exactly what I needed to see. I was hopeful that our meeting would go just like this. Where do you feel most comfortable sitting down so we can talk about what it looks like to partner?

See what I did there? What's the answer most commonly going to be when I asked that question? Kitchen table, dining room, living room. Let's just say they say kitchen table and sit down at the table. Now is the perfect time to transition into the Time and Money Presentation.

## The Time and Money Presentation

This is the same presentation each and every time. I always say let's talk about price first because it's usually what's most important to people, but before we do, give me your real price, the price that you guys really want to sell for. I've done a little bit of research here. I've done some digging, I know what prices were in the boom. I also knew what prices were in the bust. Based on that, I figure you're pretty educated on the market with the Internet and world that we live in.

**Money**

**Where do you really need to be on price?**

Now I must stop right there and talk about the 10-listing rule. Here is what it is. When you get to 10 listings, you earn the right to say no to any deal. Otherwise you take the listing. Everything up to 10 is a learning and working opportunity.

When they say $450,000, here's your response.

Perfect. That's a good starting point. I can work with that. That's exactly what I was hoping that you would say so we are in the same ballpark on price.

**Time**

Then we go to the next question.

The next question is a little bit more important because it's going to determine if I want to do business with you and I think ultimately will determine if you guys want to do business with me.

They're going to think, what's this question? Right?

But I must ask you this question. The question is time, but I have to ask you the question in a way that you'll understand what I'm saying. So, let me ask you if tomorrow morning I brought you a price and terms that you are willing to accept, could you guys move in the next 30 days?

The psychology of this is what I am doing when I'm giving this presentation. I'm being assumptive that I am their choice. I say the following in my head to give me the confidence that I need them to feel:

*I am the best choice that money can buy. I can do this. This is what I do. I'm a network to these people. This is what we specialize in. There's no need for them to start shopping. They're done. They've stopped shopping in their mind at this point.*

When I asked them that, there are typically three responses. This is the equivalent of teaching a canine dog how to bite and what's more important than teaching a canine dog how to bite? Teaching a canine dog to do what? Release. Exactly.

I'm going to teach you how to get them hooked and how to release them if it's not a good fit. Here's what we have. There are three responses.

**Response 1:**

**Seller(s):**
My first response I love, this is my favorite one, but the sellers will look at each other and say:
Are you kidding me? Absolutely. Thirty days, you know what? We'll call Jimmy and Tommy to get a van over here. We can have all this stuff gone. We can move. We can be out of here in 10 days.

**Agent:**

You know what? Perfect. That's exactly what I needed to hear because you're my kind of people and that's what I do. I needed to find out if you guys were really serious about selling and I think you are, and I believe that at this point you've decided you want to do business with me because I know I've decided I want to do business with you. Now let's go ahead and look at the partnership agreement. (i.e. listing agreement)

**Response 2:**

**Seller(s)**

Response number two is what I call Tony the tough guy. Have you ever come across Tony the tough guy? I bet you have in one way or another. They will say:
I don't need to sell. What do I want to sell for, I don't care? I honestly don't care if it ever sells, I don't care.

**Agent:**

You know what Mr./Mrs. Seller I really appreciate you. I appreciate you a lot. I appreciate you more than you know. I asked that question for a reason, see, I don't know if I told you at the beginning, but I'm a selling agent. I'm not a listing agent. A listing agent can afford to tell you what you want to hear. They can afford to keep your property on the open market for the next 365 days while they go on to sell 14 other properties. I cannot. My reputation is tied to getting this one sold. I really appreciate your time and for being upfront that this is not something you're looking to do right away because I prioritize people based on the need and the ability to be able to move.

I'll tell you what I'm going to do for you, I'm going to go to my office. I have an amazing office and we have some amazing real estate professionals who are listing agents. I'm going to find who right now is accepting new business and I'm going to refer you to them. Do yourself a favor, if I get one of the top agents to come out here and meet with you, don't blow it. Okay?

Now if I walk off, what could potentially happen as I'm walking away to the door? I've had a lot of Tony the tough guys say, Hey, wait a minute Mike, sit down. If they don't pull me back and I make it all the way to the door, then I get in my truck and drive back to the office. When I get there, I find somebody in my office that I can give the listing to. I would tell them I went on a listing appointment and I got the seller all teed up. I can't take them right now, it's not a good fit for me. So why don't we do this? I'll refer them to you for a thirty percent referral. What do you think? All you have to do is show up, look good and slam dunk the listing.

What will typically happen is that the agent will go out, take the listing, and then take the ballpeen hammer every month and keep lowering the price down. They will get the price down as listing agents are skilled at doing just that.

The listing agent will finally get the price where it needs to be and then the property will sell. I'll make 30 percent for my time and efforts. I'm always going to try to help you monetize your time and effort so that if you're actually going out and talking to people and you're going on appointments, no matter which way it turns out, I could show you how to make money in many ways in real estate.

**Response 3:**

**Seller(s):**

Now let's go with my third response to the time question. This one takes a little bit of skill. This is typically the sweet elderly couple and yes, I said that. The sweet elderly couple. They're looking at you when you said that, remember what I said right? If I bring you an offer with pricing terms that you're willing to accept tomorrow morning, can you go ahead and move in 30 days? This sweet couple look at each other. They are communicating without words.

They're having a panic attack together, right? They have the deer in the headlights look and they're thinking, oh man, we have knickknacks and patty whacks and things that have shoved into closets for 33 years here and everywhere. Does he not understand? And then they could have a physical or emotional reaction from something that you said. Here's where you must watch this, you have to be able to understand this situation and you must be able to catch people as they're falling. Then you have to swoop in to provide a safety net.

**Agent:**

You can counter with. Actually, you know what, it could take 30 to 90 days to secure the right buyer for your home. Also, as the seller you are in control. We could extend the closing another 30 or 45 days. Even beyond that if need be. And by the way, I know a lot of movers and I have some really good ones who are really meticulous and with carefully pack your items.

What I'm going to do is this, I'm going to come alongside of them, like a partner, because I know they're having a physical disruption of words about what I said about selling the home. Not only selling it but selling it quickly. The key is to always pay attention to what your sellers are saying and even watch their body language. It will help you better engage and form a solid relationship with them to move forward with a deal. Moving forward after the response. I say:

That's exactly what I needed to hear you say today because this is exactly the house, we need for our inventory. We can sell this; we can get this sold. I think at this point, based on your answers, I definitely want to partner with you. I believe perhaps you decided you'd like to partner with me, and I would like to go over what the partnership agreement looks like. I do a little head nod to get them also nodding their head. So now when they say yes. Do they all say yes? No, but there is going to be a percentage of them that do. That's my point.

I don't know how long that took. But realistically you want to keep this short and sweet. You do not want to waste your time or the sellers time. The actual presentation is not a two and a half hour or three-hour presentation. I have found that forty-five minutes to an hour should be effective.

Can I tell you something that the world doesn't want anymore? They don't want you to come in with your unicorn and rainbows and the smoke and mirrors and all the music and the national anthem playing. When you walk in, they don't care. You know what they're concerned with.

What could you do for me?

I'm giving you the easiest script of confidence that you could walk in there with and let them know and project to them, I'm the one that is here, I'm here to get this done.

Now I want to take you through the partnership agreement.

## The Partnership Agreement

First of all, what is the partnership agreement? It's a listing agreement. Sometimes people are like, wow, there's something new. There's a partnership agreement. No, I did not create something new, I just rename things. Why, because the listing agreement sounds like you're going to put me in a reverse chokehold. And some of you, the way that you look at people, I mean even the way you speak, it could really come across as a reverse chokehold.

Before we get too deep, I want to cover a common objection that comes up during the partnership presentation.

**Objection: I had another agent come out and they can do it for 5%.**

**Your Response:**
You know what, I can totally appreciate that. I'm not sure that I would want to do it at five percent. I'm a little different. I don't know if I told you, but I'm not a listing agent, I am a selling agent. So, I spend all my focus on getting the property sold within the next 30 days. I tap into my network of the top 20 percent of people in (Your County) that are always selling property. Oftentimes we call each other before it even hits the open market. Now, I have programs and commissions

that range from five and a half to ten percent. What I don't do is, I don't pick the commission for you. I let you set the commission. Before you do that, I'd like to go ahead and give you a couple options on why some people choose 7, 8, 9 or even 10 percent. Would that be okay?

What you are doing here is acknowledging the other agents offer and then showing what you can do. You are price anchoring with the higher commission levels, and you are letting them choose the level of service that they want.

This way they still feel like they're winning. If you take a listing at 5.5 percent, I would always take two and a half and pay out three percent. I never take more as a listing agent than I pay out period.

By the way, you run your own business, you are independent contractors, whatever you do, I totally support you. It's your business but look at this with a long game mindset Don't cross the ethics line, but other than that, I don't care what you do in your own individual business, but for me, I'm going to be here for the next 20 or more years. I'm looking at long term versus short term. I always pay out more. You know why? So, the next time I get a listing and it goes on the MLS I don't have one agent out there going, yeah, we are not showing that dude's listings. If you don't think that happens and you haven't been in the industry long enough. It's the truth. Maybe no one else will get real with you on this.

What I would say to the seller is because they're all going to say to you, Really 10 percent commission? Well, I like to start off with the 10 percent program because it's the most popular. That is because it's the most talked about. Doesn't mean that it's always the one that they pick, but it's the most popular because everybody wants to talk about it. I would like to talk to you about my 10 percent commission program because it's the most popular. On the 10 percent program, I pay out six percent to the cooperating brokers and I keep 4.

There's a lot of things that go into the marketing efforts behind the scenes of the home that I do upfront to make sure that we're getting professional photos and that they are staged correctly and anything else you offer. However, I want you to understand the psychology of this. Do you realize that real estate agents are not employees who receive salaries but yet their strictly commission income? That means they only eat and feed their families when they sell homes.

There might even be a few agents from other counties that will drive just a little bit into this county because they want to show your home to their potential buyers. They might be doing this because they are getting double commission on this home.

I will convey this to the seller and let them know that sometimes the increase in traffic could cause multiple offers which could drive the price up.

Now if that's not something you feel comfortable with, I do have a nine percent program. There's obviously a few more things that as we go up in price that I'm able to do with marketing based on the fact that we're receiving more commission.

There are some things that we may not be able to do. For example, maybe at the nine percent were not able to do the staging. We're not able to do that so you will come up with what you will be doing. You have to make it like a menu service.

I would say at nine percent we actually pay out five percent. So, at five percent paid to co-op we're now paying them an additional two percent more than any other listing. Now if you're a seller and I just gave you that presentation, did you consider changing your mind? Did you consider paying the 10 percent? That's my point you lose 100% of the time you don't try.

Do you get that Mr./Mrs. Seller? And they say, oh no. I mean, yeah, I guess I knew that but hearing you say it like that it's very different. Yes. What I like to do is I like to offer double what everybody else in the county is offering because if everyone else is paying a co-op 3% or less we are offering out 6%. You offer out six percent to co-op. What do you think happens? We actually get everybody. We get the whole real estate crew in the county and we bring them to your property, and they become our leverage force. Even if they have people who are slightly outside of the area that we're in, they're going to bring those people to come and take a look.

My point on commission is there is no set pricing that I or anyone have. Tailor the commission and price to help the seller sell for top dollar in the shortest time.

Now we got the yes and I am going to pull out the listing agreement and I'm going to prepare the partnership agreement. People are going to get nervous, but when you say, what I'd like to do now is review the partnership agreement with you, so you can see what it looks like to partner with me and then we can go ahead and tie this up today. We can tie up the required paperwork today and then my office or my team will come out and they'll take pictures and take care of everything else. By the way, if you don't have a team yet, who's your team?

Let's address something right now. You may be saying, Hey Mike, I am a solo agent, I don't have a team. You are your team. Okay? If I'm on a listing appointment in today's market and I'm competing with all these big teams out there, when I walk in, it's only me, right? I'm going to say this to them.

Once we take care of the partnership agreement today, we can then go ahead and get everything into the system, get it uploaded, and schedule everything else. My team will come back out to complete any other needed docs, order the aerial photos and take the interior / exterior photos and put the lockbox on and go over any other last-minute details with you. Okay?

Then later that week when I show up, I'm going to say, well actually, I happened to be in the neighborhood, and I want to take care of you personally. So, I'm here to take photos and do the different things. You are the team until you get big enough to start one.

It is all in the delivery and presentation. You most likely have a support system around you with your office. If you position yourself in the right manner it will better help you gain the trust of your sellers. Right place, right people, right time.

## Building the Business

Your whole real estate practice is going to be built on following up with people and maintaining your sphere of influence along with all of your past clients.

That book of business becomes your business and it can become a business that at some point when you decide to retire that you can sell. You want them to be your client for life. You don't want just that one sale. You want all of their sales, right? That's important, but that's only thinking on one level. You want to maintain that relationship because you want all their friends, their family, their people, the people that they know, the people that they work with. And that's the truth. This is where working the database and working your actual business comes into play.

I always try to give you action items so that you improve your business just from reading this book.

## Your Number

The first thing you need to do is to come up with your number. I want you to think of your number. I could give you a number, but you should have a number of listings that you believe that you can maintain that could become what you carry. I'm not talking about one time; this is what you carry consistently.

I'm going to give you my number. I don't expect you to adopt my number. I think you should adopt what your mind will believe. My mind truly believes that this is exactly what I would do if I chose to leave leadership and be an agent solely.

I've wrote this business plan for it. I have a 12-month model. Exactly what I would do. I would go out and get 100 listings. I would start in the southern part of Palm Beach County, which is the Boca and Boynton Beach area and I would work my way up north through Palm Beach County all the way to Jupiter, Tequesta, all the way to the Martin County line and I would talk to every single for sale by owner that wants to sell their house.

Between those county lines, I would let them know that I'm the best option money can buy to partner with. I would come in with a least a 45 minute or less presentation just like I gave you and I would bank on a numeric algorithm that if I do it enough times, then a certain amount of people would say, yes, would you agree?

Now I'm terrible at paperwork and I am not the greatest at technology, but here's the cool thing. If you go on this mission towards your number, I don't care what your number is. It could be 10, it could be 20, could be 50.

Whatever your number is, you can take these listings that you've accumulated, and you can put them in a pile.

Actually, there's people that you can pay now to put them in the MLS, so you don't even have to prepay. You can pay them when the deal closes. That's total leverage. You could pay people to take the pictures. You can pay people to go out and put lockboxes on, what you really have to get skilled at is going out and getting whatever your number is on actual listing appointments.

I had already mapped it out. It's about a 90-day binge that I would have to go on. It's called the listing binge. You know, some people binge on drugs and alcohol. I would binge on listings. I would go and make it a point to talk to every single FSBO.

Now, what do you think would happen if I talked to 100 for sale by owners? Would some of them say yes. Sure, even if I'm terrible, some could even pity me. What would happen if I follow up every week until one of three things happen?

One, they sell the property, right? Stop calling.

Two, they list with another realtor. You stop calling and I always say something positive because I believe that it will come back to you. I'm sure you chose somebody fabulous. I'm sure that was an excellent choice. I wish you the best of luck. If it doesn't work out, please feel free to call my cell phone, but just know that I'm rooting for you and I hope that you sell it.

Three is if they tell you to stop calling him because they're going to call the police. That's probably a good time to stand down.

If you do that with those 100 people that you talk to, how many more of those would actually come over time? The first week, the second week, the third week. You know, I am not of the belief that you're going to go out tomorrow morning and you're going to talk to 50 people and you're going to get 50 listings.

But here's what I know. If you go out, you take the action. Something will happen. If you're walking this way and you're going towards the goal, this could potentially happen.

But guess what usually happens, you bang a hard left or a hard right and you're over here and you're doing business over there because you put energy and focus in this direction. It doesn't always go straight to success. It's okay. You're going to veer off a little bit. It's not a big deal, but you're still going to be taking action.

I would just challenge you. Let me be in the back of your head. Every time you get soft, you get weak , you're not sure, and you don't believe in yourself thinking they are saying no, remember you can do this. You can keep going. Just hit your number. Stop making it about all the things that your brain wants to make it about.

Get rid of the white noise and don't listen to negative self-talk. Listen to what you need to accomplish and if my number is 50 and until I get to 50, I don't have time for anything. I don't have time for this. I don't have time for that.

When I was in the building mode, I never took days off. Coming up, I was not taking any time off and I was not figuring out what I could do to have fun. There was no fun. It was go time. It's build time.

Now when you get to your number, reward yourself, do something just for you. I don't even care what it is. Don't tell anybody what it is, just do something awesome. Do it. But figure out what your number is and then focus on it every single day until you get it.

Let's look at some numbers to get you motivated. If I have 100 listings, how many of them are going to sell in today's market? Give me a number, probably 90, right in today's market. But let's say I'm not great at pricing, even at

50 percent, even though I'm a little off at pricing, they are probably going to sell.

Focus all efforts in between to get each property priced to sell. Place your clients needs above yours and the money will come.

What do I do now? Here's what I do, I have to go get 50 more. And by the way, I don't think all 50 will sell at once, but I think maybe 20-22 will. Then you have to go back out and you have to keep going.  I chose 100 because I have a huge life and I have massive goals and they are pretty weird, cool, freaky things that I still want to do before my time is done.

I want big, right? I want a hundred, but your goal could be 10 and you can live a pretty good life if you put 10 listings in today's market. I'll take this algorithm as Gospel.

If 9 out of 10 sells, what's the average price of property? Let's use $200k to be conservative. Now that price could be different in your market. We have $200k times 3%, that's $6k for each home. Now if I were to sell the 90 that would be 90 times $6k, that equals $540,000.

Can you live a good life on $540,000 thousand? Is that possible or is that not possible? I think it's totally possible. Can I give you some evidence? We do that almost every month in just one of my offices. Look at your stats. Go check your own numbers. We already do it. It's already being done. How much are you getting right now?

The real reason we don't do this is because most of us don't show up for ourselves. Most of the time we're not coming in daily, we're not pouring into our business. We don't take the first 15-20 minutes of every single day and try this: I'm just going to be purposeful today. I'm going to block out everything else and then I'm just going to grind and I'm going to make contact with people. I'm going to get appointments, and some of those appointments are going to say yes. They're going to list with you.

What do you think? If you give one year, give me one year of your life, 12 months, let's do 12 months together. Let's walk together for 12 months and you take 15 minutes every single day. Whether you like it or not, you're sick and tired or whatever, you still take 15 minutes anyway.

You don't feel good. Sorry. You got a tummy ache. Doesn't matter. You take the 15 minutes. Something bad happened in life. Sorry, 15 minutes anyway. You can feel bad later. Are you with me? Here is what happens to you over the course of a year if you're going on five appointments a week, just five, five is like part time. But if you go on five appointments a week, what happens to you after one year? You're a different individual. Right? And we're all totally different individuals. You Rise! And then you Rise again, begin with a whole new next level you. You are on your way to becoming the grandest version of the highest vision you have ever held of yourself.

# The FSBO Skit

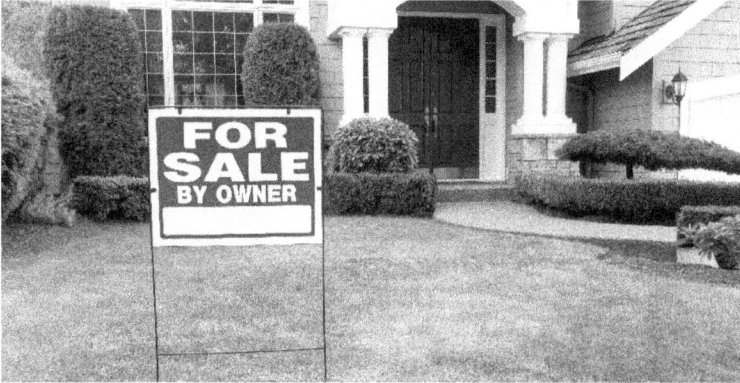

Now I'm going to give you my skit; I discovered early on that I was terrible on the phone, so it forced me to go out and meet people in person. I was on the phones and even guys and gals in my own office would say, "Mike, you should really stop making calls."

## Step 1 – Scouting

So here's what I would do. I would go out in neighborhoods and look for the for sale by owner properties. Usually they would have a sign in the yard that said: For Sale by Owner. I would park my car in the street parallel or perpendicular to the door. I would leave the car door open; I would leave the car running. When I would walk up to the door, I would knock on it and then I would roll back about 15 feet. Which by the way, this helps for a good getaway in case you run into a creeper. You have a 15-foot lead on anybody, you better be able to beat them, or we need to have a different coaching session. With a 15-foot lead, you better be able to get in the car before they can get you. It also removes their thinking of, who's coming to my door, who's knocking at the door, right?

Yes. Stranger danger. I'm already on the balls of my feet. I think it takes down all the energy so that they can come in and say, you know what, I appreciate this, somebody is here but he's not staring into my window. Not doing the whole glare down, waiting for them. If I do this, they might be more apt to answer the door.

## Step 2 – Making Contact

They come to the door and they say hello and you say with excitement, "You're here! Fantastic. Is the home still for sale? Well, yes it is. Perfect. I have to meet some folks around the corner, but I'd love to come back by and take a tour of your home."

I can hand them my business card, or I can say I took a picture of the little red and white sign with your number. But mainly I'm going to be excited about the house from the looks of the outside. I definitely want to see the inside. I can't meet with you now. I have to meet with some folks around the corner, but I'm going to come back or I'll call you and we'll set up a time for me to come by. They shut the door. I drive off.

Don't squeal your tires. Don't drive on the lawn. Now you tell me, what did we just do? What did we create with this potential person that wants to sell their home?

It's a warm contact to follow up. They've already seen my face. We've already had a little bit of connectivity. What else? You have a client already, I didn't say I had a client, right? Because I don't ever put myself inside a trick box that I can't get out of. But I inferred it, didn't I? With my energy. They're thinking it could be a client. What else? Mystique. I'm interested. I want to know more. Let's talk to this guy. I don't know, there's something about it. I want to meet to find out more, right? What else?

Maybe there's something else. It kind of felt like there was something here. It is perceived value because they think that you can help them sell their house. I never even said it, but I did infer. That's what you picked up, right? Yes. We are giving energy that I'm your guy/gal. Who else was doing that? How many people actually go out and meet FSBO's in person?

## Step 3 – Getting the Appointment

Let me tell you something, I had no family here. I had no friends. I was 21-22 years old when I came into the business, I was a pup. I knew who I was going to talk to and so I would go out and talk to for sale by owners. Then I was on the phone with them, at first, I was terrible. I got in my car and would start driving and having these discussions with myself.

Did I create urgency, are they feeling a sense of urgency to meet with me and talk to me and find out what. What was that all even about or let's say it was the wife and the husband wasn't home. Now when the husband gets home, the wife and husband are going to have a talk, do you think that talk is going to go something like this? I think I found our realtor®. We have to meet with this guy. I don't know. He kind of came by today. It was like Flash Gordon in and out, right?

Or say it was the husband and his wife comes home. Honey, remember how we said we weren't going to talk to any realtors®? I think we should just talk to this one. I think this guy is working with a bunch of people and I think we should. I think we should actually take a meeting.

Now when I call, that is a lot easier of a call for me then cold calling off of a list from Zillow or what have you. Now I pick up the phone and say, how are you doing? This is Michael. I came by the other day. I didn't have time to actually stop right then and there, but I'd love to see your home. When is a good time for me to take a 15-minute walk through of your home?

## Step 4 – Getting the Listing

Once I have the appointment set, I use the Getting the Listing method that I showed you in the earlier chapter. You don't have to complicate this process. It is a system and not just a system a proven system that has worked over and over again.

That right there, that little skit turned into about $200,000 a year in real estate commissions for me. My first sale was $87,500. It was 1404 Amaryllis Avenue in Victoria Woods in West Palm Beach, Florida, 33415. Her name was Kari. She was my first client ever. We're still friends today. She loved me and I loved her. It was amazing.

I remember going to the closing table and getting my check, I was with Re/Max, so things were a little bit different. It was $87,500 so my check after splits was around $1,222 bucks. I looked at that check for several hours and I thought, I'm going to have to sell a lot of houses.

Now before that I was in the mobile home industry and we'd sell a mobile home for $50,000. Where on average you can make five grand in commission. That was the commission on selling the mobile home. So, to sell an $87,500 home and make $1,222, plus I had to pay my broker $900 a month whether I sold a home or not. Right? That was part of my monthly deal. I paid $900 a month in fees and that was my mortgage payment back then. I thought everybody did it. I had a high level of respect for all realtors.

## Wrap Up

Here is my action item. We talked about setting your number earlier. Now is the time to do that.

I want you to pick a number. Not just any number I want you to pick the number of listings that you want to have consistently. It does not matter what the number is, but I would challenge you to pick a safe number and then increase it by at least 10%. You should always strive to better yourself and reach farther than you think you can.

Once you have your number, I want you to first write it down and then share it with every single person that you know, that it is your number. I want you to go on a mission and say, this is my number. I don't care what your number is, I love your number. Whatever your number is, I totally respect it. I want you to come up with your number and then I want a commitment to it.

Then from this point on, I want you to go out every single day and I want you to take action towards that number. That number is going to be the number of listings that you can see yourself carrying in your business, you must visualize this, you have to see this.

Your listing inventory will become your focus. It's going to be a business build that could take anywhere from three months to a year because it's going to be a big number, right? Once you get to that number, your new life mission is, as you sell them, you replace them to maintain that active number of listings to give you the life and money to fund it.

I want you to take action from this book. Come up with your number, tell everybody you know what your new number is every single day, say, I'm a real estate professional and when you put a name badge on, and when you suit up as a real estate agent. You put a laser focus on each day to obtain your number of active listings. Each day you have to take a little bit of action towards getting to this goal.

This focus on listings will propel you through just about any market. It will in turn give you the money you need to fund your perfect life. You will have to Rise and Rise again as you meet new challenges or even as you smash your life goals. Knowing where you want to go will always help you Rise and Grind one more time. I believe in you, do you?

# The Scripts

## Getting the Appointment

**Agent:** Hi, this is YOUR NAME. I'm with YOUR COMPANY I was calling to find out if your home is still for sale.

**Seller(s):** Yes, it is.

**Agent:** Okay, fantastic. I'd love to come and take a look at it. I'm going to be in your area between three and five. When will be a good time for me to come by?

## Getting the Listing

I have a little speech when I first come in and I always say:

**Agent:** Hey, you know what? I'm not a listing agent. I'm a little different. I'm a selling agent. I know you probably heard from about six or seven other realtors® who are probably skilled listing agents, but I'm a little different. I'm a selling agent.

You see, I'm networked to the top 20 percent of people who push property in (Your County), and typically we call each other when we're looking for things so that we can find matches quicker. That is why I'm here today, I'm here to look and see if this is something that I can really get sold because I partner with an exclusive few people just like you if we're a match.

So, what I figured we'd do is you would take me on a tour, show me the house just like you would as if I were a buyer. And then after that we can sit down and talk about what it would look like to partner together. Cool.

**Seller(s):** Great

**Agent:** Now, would you do me a favor? Would you tour me through the home as if I were the buyer? Then you can point out all the different things that you've done.

After the viewing and you are ready to sit down:

**Agent:** This is fantastic. This is exactly what I needed to see. I was hopeful that our meeting would go just like this. Where do you feel most comfortable sitting down so we can talk about what it looks like to partner?

## The Time and Money Presentation

**Agent:** Where do you really need to be on price?

**Seller(s):** We would need to get $450,000.

**Agent:** Perfect. That's a good starting point. I can work with that. That's exactly what I was hoping that you would say so we are in the same ballpark on price.

**Agent:** The next question is a little bit more important because it's going to determine if I want to do business with you and I think ultimately will determine if you guys want to do business with me.

But I must ask you this question. The question is time, but I have to ask you the question in a way that you'll understand what I'm saying. So, let me ask you if tomorrow morning I brought you a price and terms that you are willing to accept, could you guys move in the next 30 days?

**Response 1:**

**The seller(s):** Are you kidding me? Absolutely. Thirty days, you know what? We'll call Jimmy and Tommy to get a van over here. We can have all this stuff gone. We can move. We can be out of here in 10 days.

**Agent:** You know what? Perfect. That's exactly what I needed to hear because you're my kind of people and that's what I do. I needed to find out if you guys were really serious about selling and I think you are, and I believe that at this point you've decided you want to do business with me because I know I've decided I want to do business with you. Now let's go ahead and look at the partnership agreement.

**Response 2:**

**The seller(s):** I don't need to sell. What do I want to sell for, I don't care. I honestly don't care if it ever sells, I don't care.

**Agent:** You know what Mr./Mrs. Seller I really appreciate you. I appreciate you a lot. I appreciate you more than you know. I asked that question for a reason, see, I don't know if I told you at the beginning, but I'm a selling agent. I'm not a listing agent. A listing agent can afford to tell you what you want to hear. They can afford to keep your property on the open market for the next 365 days while they go on to sell 14 other properties. I cannot. My reputation is tied to getting this one sold. I really appreciate your time and for being upfront that this is not something you're looking to do right away because I prioritize people based on the need and the ability to be able to move.

I'll tell you what I'm going to do for you, I'm going to go to my office. I have an amazing office and we have some amazing real estate professionals who are listing agents. I'm going to find who right now is accepting new business and I'm going to refer you to them. Do yourself a favor, if I get one of the top agents to come out here and meet with you, don't blow it. Okay?

**Response 3:**

**The seller(s):** They're having a panic attack together, right? They have the deer in the headlights look and they're thinking, oh man, we have knickknacks and patty whacks and things that have shoved into closets for 33 years here and everywhere. Does he not understand? And then they could have a physical or emotional reaction from something that you said. Here's where you must watch this, you have to be able to understand this situation and you must be able to catch people as they're falling. Then you have to swoop in to provide a safety net.

**Agent:** Actually, you know what, it could take 30 to 90 days to secure the right buyer for your home. Also, as the seller you are in control. We could extend the closing another 30 or 45 days. Even beyond that if need be. And by the way, I know a lot of movers and I have some really good ones who are really meticulous and with carefully pack your items. Moving forward after the response. I say:

**Agent:** That's exactly what I needed to hear you say today because this is exactly the house, we need for our inventory. We can sell this; we can get this sold. I think at this point, based on your answers, I definitely want to partner with you. I believe perhaps you decided you'd like to partner with me, and I would like to go over what the partnership agreement looks like.

# Potential Objections

**Do I have to pay a commission?**

Response:

You know what? I'm not sure I'd want to pay a commission either. I just know I'd really love to see your home. I'm going to be in the area today between three and five. What works for you? I want to take a quick 15-minute look at the house.

**I have been burned by a real estate professional before.**

Response:

Yep, I could see that you feel you were burned somehow by a real estate agent before, but I know I'd really like to come and look at the house. I'm going to be in the area today between three and five. What works for you? I want to take a quick 15-minute look at the house.

**I am frustrated that five or six agents have already called me.**

Response:

You know what? I can see where you may be frustrated by that. I heard a lot of my colleagues are also calling. I'm part of the inventory team here at Keller Williams, so that would make sense. I'd really love to come and see your house. I'm going to be in the area today between three and five. What works for you? I want to take a quick 15-minute look at the house.

**Do you have a buyer?**

Response:

You know what? I'm glad you brought that up. I work with about 67 families a month at my office through this network / team that we have. And right now, we're out looking at other inventory that's not yet on the open markets, which kind of brings me exactly to this phone call and why I'd like to meet with you. I'm going to be in your area today between three and five. Do you think that we could possibly set up a 15-minute interview or a run through, so I can look at your house?

**I have friends who are realtors®.**

Response:

I totally understand. I have friends who are in real estate too. I'm not sure I'd want to do business with them either, but I know I'd love to come and look at your home. When would be a good time for a 15-minute run through?

**I had another agent come out and they can do it for 5%.**

Response:

You know what, I can totally appreciate that. I'm not sure that I would want to do it at five percent. I'm a little different. I don't know if I told you, but I'm not a listing agent and the selling agent. So, I spend all my focus on getting the property sold within the next 30 days. I tap into my network of the top 20 percent of people in (Your County) that are always selling property. Oftentimes we call each other before it even hits the open market. Now, I have programs and commissions that range from five and a half to ten and a half percent. What I don't do is, I don't pick the commission for you. I let you set the commission. Before you do that, I'd like to go ahead and give you a couple options on why some people choose 7, 8, 9 or even 10 percent. Would that be okay?

# About "*The General*" Michael Brue

Michael Brue specializes in helping professional's break down the walls of mediocrity and get on a proven path to growth and success. His life work is helping people meet their maximum future self!

He has been a top Real Estate Broker and General Manager for close to 16 years using his expertise to help build and expand five Keller Williams Realty Market Centers in South Florida. Michael now leads a team of 1,100 plus Realtors© spread across seven locations that have generated several billion dollars in volume. He is passionate about building others up and allowing them to shine with the success he knows is inside of them.

Using his proven system, he is able to draw out anyone's maximum potential.

KW Palm Beaches, KW Jupiter, KW Treasure Coast, KW Palm City, KW Port St Lucie, KW Vero Beach and the Island of Vero Beach.

For more information on how Michael can help you with your business or real estate career, visit his site at MichaelBrue.com.

THEGENERAL

www.ingramcontent.com/pod-product-compliance
Lightning Source LLC
Chambersburg PA
CBHW060633210326
41520CB00010B/1590